BURT REYNOLDS
PORTRAIT OF A SUPERSTAR
by Dianna Whitley

Publishers · GROSSET & DUNLAP · New York
A FILMWAYS COMPANY

Acknowledgment and thanks for the help
and support of Kathy Breslin, Peggy Casey,
Marsha Daly, Bill Honan, Delia and David
Jones, Robin Leach, Bill Martin, Diana Price,
Dan Rosenblatt, and Bob Young.

For Damian, Sarah-Beth, and Kelle

Cover photo: © C. Brownie Harris/Black Star
Copyright © 1979 by Dianna Whitley
Published simultaneously in Canada
Library of Congress catalog card number: 78-73640
First printing 1979
ISBN: 0-448-15479-X
Printed in the United States of America

Design by Joyce Schnaufer

CONTENTS

After years of playing second fiddle, Burt has been one of the top ten box-office draws for the past six years, and now is number one in the country.

1/THE AURA OF A SUPERSTAR

Scene: Upper East Side, New York. Two blocks are lined with panel trucks, vans, and trailers. The sequel to *An Unmarried Woman*, called *Starting Over*, is being filmed, and it stars Burt Reynolds.

The door to one of the buildings opens and Reynolds walks out quickly, flanked by no less than five bodyguards. He looks tired, and a little older than one would expect, but when he smiles and says something to the man next to him, the fatigue is instantly gone and he looks as young and handsome as he ever has. Two women timidly approach him, Instamatics and autograph books in hand. It has been a long, rugged day, but he stops and poses for a picture with a little boy who is speechless with adulation, and signs his autograph with a graciousness that is rarely seen in a celebrity. Anyone watching the scene can tell immediately that he likes people—especially children.

In a moment, he is gone, having disappeared into a red-and-white trailer truck. It is a $60,000 piece of equipment outfitted with a shower, kitchen, two color TV's,

beds, living-room furniture, and several phones, and it has been brought from California for Reynolds' use. He is taking a nap—or simply refuge—inside.

Several women gather round the back of the truck where he is lying down, inches away, and there is excitement in the air just knowing he is *there*. "Is Burt Reynolds *REALLY* in there?" a latecomer asks. She immediately joins the others, who are clearly planning to wait in the rain to get a glimpse of him.

It is a quiet street, and it is raining, so not much of a crowd forms. There are policemen and bodyguards everywhere to make sure there is no trouble. The driver is talking to one of the cops, telling him about the time some over-enthusiastic fans nearly turned the trailer over in an effort to get to him, and about another time when word got out that he was filming in Brooklyn and a mob of three thousand showed up. There isn't that kind of frenzy today—they have kept the site of the filming very quiet this time—but there is a charge in the air that is unmistakable.

Burt has the kind of animal magnetism that you can feel across a room.

The bodyguards pass the time by telling anecdotes to one another. A photographer strikes up a conversation with one of them. She asks if there is any chance she can get a shot of Burt and Candice Bergen together. He senses she wants the shot because she has heard the rumor that they are Hollywood's newest Hot Item, and not simply because they are in the same movie. He tells her firmly that Candice has finished shooting and will not be around.

"It seems a shame that every time two beautiful people work together, everybody comes to the wrong conclusion," he tells her. "I'm with him twenty-four hours a day, and I sure haven't seen anything going on," he says to dispel the rumor. "Don't people realize that he's been around beautiful women all his life? He doesn't go running after every one he meets." His affection and respect for Reynolds are obvious, and he praises Burt as an employer: "I work with them all," he says, letting her know he is not beholden to Reynolds, "and in my book, he is definitely the best. He's a really terrific guy."

Two hours pass. The group of people waiting for Burt to appear are an indication of his broad appeal. There are a handful of women of various ages, a couple of blacks, an old man, and a couple of kids. It couldn't have been set up better by his publicity department.

Finally, he comes out of the trailer and walks over to where the next scene is being shot. Again, he is gracious and

Like the pillow says—Burt loves his fans.

Burt shot *Starting Over* in New York and Boston with co-stars Mary Kay Place (shown here) and Candice Bergen.

He's not even six feet tall, but he stands out in a crowd no matter how many bodyguards surround him.

charming to everyone who approaches him, and there is nothing phoney about it. As he walks, photographers are running backward, their cameras whirring madly. Burt notices a friend of his on crutches in the direct path of one of the photographers. "Watch out, Billy," he says with quiet authority. No one else had noticed.

In seconds, he was gone again, leaving a feeling that something had *happened*.

The kind of electricity Burt exudes has to do with presence. He has a magnetism that is almost palpable—an energy you can feel across a room. Even though he is only five feet eleven and walks sandwiched by five bodyguards who are taller and broader than he is by far, his is definitely the dominating presence.

This kind of thing is called power, and there is no question about the fact that Reynolds possesses it. Magnetism and charisma and charm and an electrifying energy emanate from him like radar, affecting everyone who comes close to him. It is the stuff of which stars are made. It is the same kind of vitality with which Gable and Bogart were endowed. It is a compelling force that makes you want to get to know him, and signals a certain danger at the same time.

He is the kind of man who commands great loyalty and affection, and yet triggers off fear at the same time. You would not want to cross him. You also wouldn't want to disappoint him, because he is the kind of man you like immediately, and you would never want to let him down. And if you are a woman, he is the kind of man you might do anything just to spend a few hours with.

Burt is always gracious and warm when people ask him for an autograph.

Dianna Whitley

After years of playing second fiddle, Burt Reynolds is today, the hottest star in Hollywood. After fifteen years in the business, he became an overnight success in 1972. When he appeared as the first male nude centerfold in *Cosmopolitan* magazine, he changed instantly from a moderately successful actor to a sex symbol.

About the same time, he began revealing another part of himself—a terrifically funny personality, as exhibited on the Johnny Carson show. The two debuts boosted him from the "third Indian on the left" to a fourteen-carat-gold celebrity.

He has a fascinating mixture of qualities that make him attractive to people of all kinds, men and women alike. Tough and macho one minute, he is disarmingly vulnerable and boyish the next. He's cocky and virile, a real "Marlboro Man" who still prefers to do his own stunts, to the dismay of his producers. Yet he is

Dianna Whitley

Burt appreciates his fans' enthusiasm though once some overzealous fans nearly toppled a trailer he was in.

surprisingly old-fashioned and sentimental. Not just an outdoor man, he is extraordinarily well read, with a penchant for poetry and philosophy. He is serious and devilish, polished and rough, contemplative and down to earth, outgoing and shy. He seems completely easygoing and self-confident, but Tom Topor of *The Post* once described him as being "casual as an exposed wire, assured as a jockey on a runaway horse." Most of all, though, he is sexy—that four-letter word that sells everything from movies to Mazola.

Burt's life and public image have taken many turns along the way. During the years of too many mediocre movies and TV roles, he became an increasingly hostile and angry young man. Like many of the "he-men" he played, he would do anything to get attention, including jumping out of a window or throwing a punch. He says that he used to have such difficulty in expressing himself, the way he disagreed with someone, was to rip their shirt off.

Today, there isn't a trace of the chip that once had an almost full-time place on his shoulder. He found that he was as fast with a one-liner as he was with his fist, and that wit and charm got him a lot further than fighting.

With films like *White Lightning, Gator,* and *Hooper* he has established a new kind of movie that combines adventure and comedy, and no one is more suited to play in them than he is.

His fans are almost cultlike in their loyalty and are, in his words, "the people who can't talk back to the cops and the landlord the way my characters do."

He has been one of the top ten box-office attractions for the past six years, but *Smokey and the Bandit*, which grossed revenues second only to those of *Star Wars* in 1977, placed him irrefutably in the number-one position. His last four movies have made over $400 million in the past eighteen months.

A young fan is thrilled that Burt takes the time to pose with him.

Now that he can call his own shots, Reynolds is taking the opportunity to head in an entirely new direction. He began this new course by directing and starring in *The End,* a black comedy he helped finance, and is committed through 1982 to do films that will be more in the Cary Grant mold than the stereotype he has been confined to until now.

Eventually, he would like to put all his efforts into directing, which he describes as the "second-best sensation I've ever had." But that is getting way ahead of the story.

Burt was rebellious as a young boy. The son of a sheriff, he got into more than his share of trouble when he was a teenager.

2/"MULLET"— A TEENAGE REBEL

It is not a coincidence that Burt Reynolds became famous playing good ol' boys, for Burt is steeped in Southern ways. He was born in Waycross, Georgia, and grew up in Riviera Beach, Florida. The South is so much a part of him that he considers his 160-acre ranch in Jupiter, Florida, more his home than his baronial mansion in Beverly Hills. He goes there between movies as often as he can, and has been known to travel the backroads of the Southern states when he gets a little free time.

Burt is part Indian and part Italian: "That's why I'm so screwed up. . . . Half of me wants to grow hair and the other half doesn't." In a less comical mood, Burt's pride in his parents and his background is apparent. His family history reads like a page out of *American Heritage*. His grandmother was a full-blooded Cherokee who met Burt's grandfather when he was a forestry teacher living on the reservation. His father was born on that reservation, and has all the fire and stature of his Indian heritage. He also lived on the other

side of the fence, as a cowboy in Utah, before he met his wife to be, who was Italian.

When Burt was growing up, his father was the town sheriff, and Burt saw him as a double authoritarian figure. Many years later, when he was finally able to see him as a man, Burt was happy to give his father a chance to return to his cowboy youth by asking him to run his ranch.

As a young teenager, however, it was a different story. The hostility and arrogance that Reynolds would display in his early years in Hollywood were just beginning to bloom. By the time he was in junior high school, Burt was a wild and rebellious teenager who seemed to love three things—sports, girls, and getting into trouble.

Girls were not easy to handle when young Buddy Reynolds was first trying out his wings. He was shy around the weaker sex (who he wasn't so sure were really weaker) until he got a little older and quite a bit bolder. Sports were a much easier area for him to handle, for he was a born

The Silver Screen Archives

When he was in junior high, Burt was terrified of girls, but by the time he was a senior he was already something of a ladies' man.

athlete. And getting into trouble was something he excelled at in his early teens. Burt was naturally rebellious, but the fact that his father was the sheriff only further heated the resentment boiling inside his head. Being the son of a police chief is like being the son of a preacher—everyone expects you to be a model child. The normal course of action is in the opposite direction, and Burt was no exception.

He and his father became like two stags with antlers locked. The older Burt (also called Buddy) was determined his son would behave the way he thought he should, and the younger Burt was equally determined to live his own life the way he wanted to, which more often than not was not at all what his authoritarian father had in mind for him. Burt set about getting into trouble at every opportunity when he was in his early teens. He joined a gang

that spent their time looking for scrapes to get themselves in and out of. Burt's father resolved that his son would not receive preferential treatment because of his own position. Therefore, when Burt and his friends once ended up in jail for fighting, Burt was the first one in—and the last one out.

Burt continued bucking authority until, at the age of fourteen, he couldn't take it anymore. He ran away from home, which resulted in a second visit to jail when he was picked up for vagrancy in a small town nearby. The police called his father, whose reaction was to tell them to keep Burt there overnight to teach him a good lesson.

Father and son were equally stubborn when Burt was released from jail. Burt, either too mad or too humiliated to go home, went to a girl friend's house to stay for a while. Neither of the Burts would give an inch. The father refused to tell his son that all was forgiven and that he was welcome back home, and the son refused to ask for the forgiveness. When they met on the street, they exchanged polite hellos, but that was all.

A year later, Burt moved back home, without either one ever having yielded. His attitude had changed, though, and for the rest of his high-school years he didn't get into any more scrapes. In fact, he got good grades, did more or less what he was told, and applied himself to doing well in sports, as his father wanted him to. The older Burt believed that a boy who used up his energy playing sports didn't have enough left over to get into trouble, and he

may have been right, since Burt was never to see the inside of a jail again.

They were not exactly a closely knit family, though. Burt may have kept out of trouble, but he also kept his distance. He is very close to his parents and his brother and sister now, but when he was growing up, he never really knew them. It wasn't until he was in his early twenties that he felt he knew his father at all. Now that he has grown up enough to be good friends with him, Burt can laugh about it. "I was amazed how much my father had learned from the time I was sixteen until I was twenty-one," he says with that familiar Reynolds humor.

While he outwardly gave in to his fa-

Casually holding a glass of champagne, leaning against his Mercedes, Burt is a class act.

ther's authority, there was one place where Reynolds always felt that he was his own man, and that was in a car. This was the one place where he could really assert himself and his masculinity. He could even do it and still seem to be obeying his father's orders by coming home on time, but doing it by speeding, especially in the last stretch, driving the car eighty-five miles an hour between the grocery store and his house—three blocks away.

He had more than his share of accidents, and even totalled three cars. (In fact, the many scars he got in car accidents would later lend a touch of realism to the opening scene of *Hooper*, as the stuntman gets dressed. As the background music builds up, the camera comes in close and examines every inch of Reynolds' body, lingering over each and every scar.) He got a ticket once for driving 105 miles an hour. It's a sure bet that wasn't the only time he drove that fast.

This kind of rebelliousness once nearly cost him his life. He was seventeen, speeding home in the rain, and he idly wondered how much the car would slide if he jerked the wheel. When he tried it and nothing much happened, he jerked it so hard it completely spun out on him. At sixty-five miles an hour, the car went out of control, and Burt was thrown onto the beach as the car barreled ahead and rammed into a coconut tree. The engine went right through the front seat.

The rebellious spirit that led Burt Reynolds to do things his own way, no matter what the cost, may have been set off by his strict father, but the anger and defiance were exacerbated when he realized that he was from the wrong side of the tracks. He found out at a very young age that while this is a free country, some people are freer, and more equal, than others.

Burt grew up in Riviera Beach, but he went to school in nearby fashionable Palm Beach, the Monte Carlo of Florida. The town he lived in was the kind of

In his sunglasses, Burt looks every inch a movie star.

working-class community in which most of the kids dropped out of school early in order to work on the fishing boats with their fathers. The kids Burt grew up with were tough, with the kind of "street knowledge" he still displays today.

Suddenly, he was thrown in with kids who were from rich, powerful families, and all too ready to point that out to him. Being from a lower-middle-class background is one thing—having that fact rubbed in your face by your classmates is quite another. And Burt's being Indian and Italian in a WASP community didn't help. He rarely talks about the subject, but he probably learned the meaning of the word prejudice at a painfully young age.

Being attractive, Burt sometimes dated girls from Palm Beach, but he remembers with a wince that when he went out with one of the budding young debutantes, he was forced to use the servants' entrance.

It was a long time ago and very far away, but he may also remember vividly the humiliation he felt when he was called names by the letter-sweater set. They called all the kids from Riviera Beach "Mullets" and "Greaseballs," and there was nothing affectionate about the nicknames. He says today that it must have been because of the way he rolled his T-shirts and put a thousand pounds of Vaseline in his hair, but it wasn't a joking matter at the time. Then he must have felt the first determination to make something of himself and prove that he was as good as everyone else, if not better. Then he must have felt the first resentment that later branded him as an angry young man in Hollywood.

Burt remembers that much of his childhood had the unreality of a movie, and recalls wishing that he could somehow stop the action and recast himself in a different part. He escaped into the make-believe world of movies, reveling in the excitement of films like *Jim Thorpe—All American* and *The Spirit of West Point*—movies about men, real men, who could do anything they wanted, say anything they wanted, and go anywhere they wanted; men who succeeded against all odds; men who had everything against them and came out on top anyway.

No one called them names like "Mullet" and made them use the servants' entrance to pick up their girl. They had the world by a string, and Burt Reynolds intended to achieve the same power.

The magic key to his independence seemed to young Buddy to be athletics. He was a natural athlete, endowed with nerve, strength, and coordination. And he was fast.

In junior high school, he won a race hands down one day, and the next day he found out what being an athlete could do for him. Some of the letter-sweater kids who had never bothered to speak to him (unless it was to call him names or throw a sandwich across the cafeteria at him) approached him in the locker room and asked him to race Vernon Rollison, the fastest kid in school. Without giving it a second thought, he agreed.

The next day, he strode across the football field to meet the challenge, and by the time he reached the goalpost, almost the entire school of four or five hundred kids had followed. He kicked his shoes off and won the race. Overnight, everything changed. He gained recognition and respect. That was the last time anyone ever called him "Mullet." From then on it was "Buddy."

He didn't need to learn the lesson twice. He may have been scared that they would bring someone he couldn't beat, or that there would be a race he couldn't win, but he knew he would always try. Anything was better than being called "Mullet." He was on his way to the kind of life he had seen in the movies. He had found the key, and he intended to use it.

There would be some races, metaphorically speaking, that he would lose—in fact, Burt would come up against some pretty hard knocks, in a few years and would need every bit of the determination that was growing inside him—but for a while he would run races, play ball, and get good grades.

If Burt found his way in the world quickly through sports, he learned equally quickly when it came to girls. At first, like all young boys, he felt tongue-tied and paralyzed around the mysterious members of the opposite sex. He watched older guys smoothly putting their arms around girls, or casually kidding with them, and was fascinated by the way they seemed to have it all, convinced that he himself would never be able to pull off those things.

Then in his junior year, everything changed for him. He fell in love with a girl named Ann Lawler, and gained the self-confidence he had been missing. Burt, a romantic from the start, heard all the proverbial bells and saw all the proverbial rockets. Ann was so terrific in every way that Burt's confidence grew just from know-

Though he raised hell in his younger days, Burt shuns the high life of Hollywood and prefers spending much of his time at home or on his ranch in Jupiter, Florida.

Burt used to watch movies all day and night when he was a kid, but never gave a thought to acting. He wanted to be a football player—thought acting was for sissies.

ing that *she* liked *him*.

By his senior year in high school, his confidence had grown so much that, he says, he became something of a Casanova. All the things he claims the press now accuses him of wrongly, he admits were true that year in high school. Smiling and relishing every moment of the memory, he says that he was "terrible," meeting one girl in the afternoon and another in the evening, going from one to the next as fast as he could. He adds wryly that even if he wanted to be that way today, he simply couldn't manage it physically. But he was young then, and it was all very new and exciting, and no power on earth could stop him from conducting his own personal Kinsey report.

Some of Reynolds' understanding of children, and people in general, comes from his keen memory of his own youth. He says that he remembers idolizing a star football player, Ned Davis, when he was

very young. He watched everything he did, including the smallest moves—how he got into his car, how he carried his school books. He worshipped him.

One day, he looked up his telephone number, and called him, just to hear his voice. When his mother answered, Burt tried to make his twelve-year-old voice as deep as he could in order to ask for Ned. When he came to the phone, as soon as Burt heard his voice on the other end of the line, he quickly hung up.

The same thing happens to Burt Reynolds today, a thousand times over, and he never gets mad. He remembers just how it felt, and why he did it, and he understands.

He also remembers the longing and the magic he felt when he went to the movies as a kid. He was so mesmerized by the people and the way they seemed to live that he spent entire days at the movie theater on weekends, going at noon and not leaving until the last show was over at eleven at night. He knew from what he saw up there on the screen that there was a lot to get out of life, and that he wanted it all. The allure of the movies captured him, and touched the part of him that was romantic and poetic, but it never occurred to him that he would someday be an actor himself. In fact, if anyone had told young Buddy Reynolds that he would grow up to be an actor, he would have laughed right in his face—if he didn't punch it first, which was a lot more likely.

By the time he was a teenager, Burt was on his way to being a man's man. His romantic, sensitive side was well hidden, probably even from himself. In school, he spent his time on football, baseball, track, and basketball. Out of school, he liked to drive fast, look at pretty girls, hunt, and raise hell with his friends. He was a teenage version of the good ol' boys who would make him famous many years down the road.

Burt's Indian heritage helped bring him an overabundance of Indian parts.

Considering the dedication that Burt displays in his profession today, it is surprising that he never thought of acting in his youth. Most actors as serious as he is about their craft have had a burning desire to be on the stage since they grew out of wanting to be firemen. Some never even go through the fireman stage—they have wanted to be actors for as long as they can remember. They staged puppet shows for their parents and took playing cowboys and Indians very seriously.

Not so with Burt Reynolds. As much as he loves being an actor today, nothing could have interested him less in high school. It wasn't until he got to college that he became interested, and that was almost by accident.

In *The Longest Yard* Burt played an ex-superstar quarterback who leads a convict football team when he finds himself in prison.

3/FROM FOOTBALL STAR TO DRAMA STUDENT

By the time he was a junior in high school, Burt's achievements in his schoolwork and on the football field had been so outstanding that his coaches and teachers suggested he apply for a football scholarship. Reynolds liked the idea, so he set about cramming three years of school into two, to meet the necessary requirements.

Since he was a good football player, the captain of his high school team, and a good student, everyone expected him to do well. Even so, the most incurable optimist could not have predicted what would happen. No less than fourteen universities offered him very tempting scholarships. Burt was flown all over the country to look over the various campuses and hear sales pitches from college officials.

Notre Dame made a very tempting offer, which he almost accepted, but he decided to stay in his home state, Florida. He signed a letter of intent at the University of Miami, but changed his mind again when he met Coach Tom Nugent at Florida State.

The coach must have been a shrewd judge of character, since he sized up Burt immediately and appealed to his greatest weakness—women. He said that while Miami must have offered him some pretty nice things, he could offer him the Florida State campus on a silver platter. When Burt didn't understand what he meant, Nugent explained that as a football player, he would be a hero—in a school where the ratio of women to men was two to one. Reynolds had his pen in hand the minute the words were spoken.

Burt enrolled in his first year of college in 1954, and it was to be one of the best years of his life. A year later, he would experience the first of many bitter setbacks, but before his troubles began, almost everything would be exactly as he wanted it to be.

College years are golden ones, the years when whole new worlds open up. All the privileges of being an adult are suddenly available. Friendships are formed that often last a lifetime. Burt loved it all.

He began school with high hopes, and they were all fulfilled. He met and made terrific friends, men and women alike. The whirlwind womanizing of his senior year in high school calmed down a bit, but he was far from lonely. One girl became so important to him that he continued visiting and keeping in touch with her for years after she married and he left college.

Burt believes that if you're going to do something, you should put your whole heart into it and really do it well. He knows that you get as much out of life as you are willing to put into it, and so he never sits back and waits for things to come to him. He works for what he gets, and works hard.

A football scholarship is no guarantee of a place on the varsity team. In fact, this is very unusual. The few freshmen who do make it to the line are *good*. And Burt Reynolds was good. He didn't sprint onto the football field a full-blown star; he became good by working hard at it every day. He was fast, he was tough, he gave it everything he had, and he wasn't afraid of anything or anyone. He showed the same courage then that he later displayed in doing his own stunt work.

All the dedication and hard work paid off. Not only did he make the varsity team, he broke a few records by making All-Florida and All-Southern Conference halfback. By the time he was a sophomore, he had been offered an option with the Balti-

At work or play, Burt always shows appreciation for the ladies.

Burt thinks a lot of the qualities that make a good football player also make a good actor.

Only when *The Longest Yard* was advertised as a "Burt Reynolds movie" did it become a hit.

more Colts. He was really on his way.

He loved playing ball so much it was almost the only thing he did that first year in college. He forgot all about the lovely coeds the coach had promised would be waiting for him. He lived, ate, and breathed football. There just wasn't time for girls —at least not much time, not enough to be a lady killer. He did have a few romances, but it was one girl at a time.

He liked to have a good time, like any college kid, but most of his energy was reserved for the thing he loved doing more than anything else in the world—playing football. He understood that this was his route out of the small-town blues. He knew that life was a big amusement park with plenty of fast rides and fun games; all you needed was a ticket to get in. Football was his ticket, and he intended to stay at the fair and use it to go on every ride.

Football also played an important role in enabling Burt to handle a lot of the emotions that were seething inside him. He got along well with people, was popular, and didn't *seem* to have any problems, but below the surface there was much confusion and anger that he didn't know how to handle. He also had an overabundance of energy sufficient for a large homemade bomb, but playing the rough and aggressive game of football kept the fuse from being lighted. After he gave up football for acting, Burt missed this outlet, and often said that he envied football players "because they are able to get all that violence out of their systems." Unfortunately, it was an outlet that would soon be cut off in the first of several disasters that left Reynolds feeling cornered with no way out.

The trouble began with a minor knee operation. It took him off the field for a while, but he had every intention of going back to playing as soon as the knee mended. He kept himself in training by going over plays mentally to keep them fresh in his mind and by doing whatever exercises he was allowed. He was counting the days until he could get back on the field.

Then one night, fate stepped in and changed the course of Burt Reynolds' life.

"One night I was driving a big Buick and got a ticket for doing ninety-five miles per hour. I remember I had the speeding ticket in one hand and was thinking how my father was going to beat the crap out of me," Burt recalls as he reflects on the night that changed everything for him. "Before I had a chance to do much of anything, I ran into a flatbed truck filled with cement blocks that was stretched across the road. Luckily my reflexes were great so I dove underneath the dashboard as the car went under the truck. The whole top of the car came off, and I was pinned inside. It took seven hours for them to get me out. My spleen was busted, but the blood had coagulated because I was bunched into a tight little ball. I didn't start hemorrhaging until they got me into the ambulance."

At the hospital, he was on the operating table for several more hours. The knee that had been mending was patched up as new as possible, but it would never be the same, and the other knee now matched it. He lost his spleen, but more than that, he lost his scholarship, and with it his dreams of being a pro. His future as a football star was over. His ticket to the fair was gone.

Many people would have been devastated by this turn of events and would feel totally justified in sinking into a deep depression, but Burt Reynolds is a born fighter. To him, a challenge is something to meet, not something to flee. His whole world had been smashed but he wasn't about to let this get the best of him.

As much as he loved football, he had come to realize that it wasn't just the game

If it hadn't been for a car accident, Burt would be a pro football player today instead of a movie star.

The Silver Screen Archives

he loved. He loved what it did for him. He loved where it took him. He loved the leverage it gave him. It made him somebody. Ever since the day he stopped being a "Mullet," he knew where he wanted to be, and it wasn't at the bottom of the heap.

Being a jock was a means to an end. He loved the means, but the end was more important. He was discovering something very important about himself, and that was that he wanted to be able to choose his lot in life. He wanted to be in the position to call the shots. The *drive* to become a top player is what was important, not the game itself. That same drive could be used in another area.

Burt still didn't know what that area would be. He had had no time to plan alternatives. All his energy had been wrapped up in what he was doing. But somewhere deep inside, he knew that he had the guts to make it in this world, and that he would. He had proved he could play ball. Now he would prove he could do something else, and he would do it just as well. He was going to be a winner.

The only trouble was he didn't have the vaguest idea of what to do. It had all been very clear to him before, but now he had to start from scratch. And even though he had the inner strength to get through, it was a terrible time for him. Everything he had been working for had suddenly been wrenched away from him, and he didn't know where to turn.

He enrolled at Palm Beach Junior College to take some courses while he recuperated from his injuries. Acting was still the furthest thing from his mind.

All his friends were still jocks, but he began noticing the group of literature and drama students who used to hang out in one part of the cafeteria. He studied them the same way he had studied his idols in junior high school. He says that they were all budding James Deans and Carroll Bakers, and that they laughed at the jocks,

Burt stumbled into being an actor, but once he did, he gave it everything he had.

but he was clearly fascinated.

He started going to some of the plays they put on for the school, and he was impressed. He began doing impersonations—at first, just to amuse his friends with imitations of Gabby Hayes and Marlon Brando, but his interest was building. Burt had always seen the world in terms of images and parts in a make-believe play. Now he was about to exchange his jock role for an actor's role. He had arrived at another crossroad, and the turn he made here would be the one that would put him on the road to where he is today.

The man who pointed out the road was someone to whom Burt is eternally grateful. This man gave Burt, still shaky and confused, the confidence he needed. His name is Watson B. Duncan III, and he was chairman of the college's English and Drama Department.

"I love this man Duncan more than anyone else in the world except my Dad. Duncan was the first to tell me: 'You'll make it, Burt!'

"But when I met him, I was really a mess.

"I'd first enrolled at Florida State University on a football scholarship. I thought I'd become All-American, and then I got injured—and that was the end of my scholarship.

"When I left Florida State and enrolled at Palm Beach Junior College, it was the low point of my life. All my dreams had been shattered. I had nowhere to go with my life.

"Then I took a course with Duncan—and he changed my entire life."

The first thing Duncan introduced Burt to was the world of books. Although he had been a good student, Burt had never really read any literature. Suddenly, he discovered a whole world, and was enthralled with everything from John Milton to Lord Byron. He says he loved it so much, he felt he *was* Lord Byron. He developed a passion for reading that has stayed with him to this day.

Duncan was a perceptive man, and he knew he had a very unusual student in his class. He spotted something in Burt that Burt himself didn't know was there. One day after class, Duncan informed Burt that he was going to be in a play. Burt told him he was crazy—he had no interest in being in a play. Duncan unperturbed, said that Burt did have an interest, whether or not he knew it.

Burt refused again, but the next day he found himself at the audition. He still didn't want to do it, but he felt a compulsion to be there. He told Duncan that he

didn't know how to read for a play, and the instructor answered by handing him the script and telling him to read. Burt got one word out, and Duncan told him he had the part.

The play was *Outward Bound*, and Burt played the moody, unhappy, gloomy character originally played by John Garfield. Burt admits it was probably type casting at the time. Nevertheless, the theatrical experience worked like a charm to get him out of the doldrums. He loved everything about it—the excitement, the attention, the applause. He said he felt like a male peacock showing off his feathers—and no one told him to stop being a showoff!

Reynolds credits Duncan with spotting the talent he didn't know he possessed. Not one to forget such things in the hot light of his present celebrity, Burt pays this tribute:

"Without this school and this man, God only knows what would have happened to me. I'll always be grateful to them. Duncan obviously saw something in me that I didn't see myself. When I realized he had faith in me—a washout—I began working hard at drama. And that's how 'Burt Reynolds, movie star' was launched!"

He showed his gratitude to his college by endowing it with a drama scholarship, which is given to a talented student each year.

Burt won an award for being the best actor in the school with his performance in *Outward Bound*. With that and Duncan's faith, Reynolds had the courage to take his first steps down the famous yellow brick road. Acting fulfilled Burt's need for attention as someone special, and it gave him a new outlet for his tremendous energy and drive. With nothing but a lot of guts, the determination to make something of himself, and the desire to do all the things he had dreamed about, he packed his bags and left for New York City.

Burt left college to try to make it as an actor in New York City, where he supported himself as a bouncer, mailman, and dishwasher.

4/DOWN AND OUT IN NEW YORK CITY

It is easy to say in retrospect that you always knew someone would make it. People do it all the time to Burt Reynolds, telling him that way back when he was first getting started, they knew he would become a star. Baloney, he says—pure and simple.

Neither he nor anyone else, with the notable exception of Watson Duncan, knew he was going to make it when he first started out. The odds are so against an aspiring actor, the most anyone could truthfully say is that he had talent, looks, and drive, which are all necessary ingredients for making it in this competitive business. The rest is hard work, perseverance, and luck. No one can tell ahead of time whether or not it will all come together into that magic formula that takes the special few to the top of the ladder, since many talented young actors get stuck on one of the rungs and never make it anywhere close.

When Burt arrived in New York, he had little money and no experience other than a season at Hyde Park Playhouse doing summer stock. On top of that, he knew no one in a city that can be overwhelming under the best of circumstances. Not only did he not have the connections to help him get through the maze that stood between him and that first important part, he didn't even know anyone who could give him friendly advice on where to live or how to make ends meet before he got the break he was looking for.

He had the money that the cement block company gave him as a settlement for his injuries, but he knew that wouldn't last long, so he did what all aspiring actors who come to New York City in search of fame and fortune do. He took a series of part-time jobs, and shared a cold-water walk-up apartment with new-found friends. Burt worked for the post office during the Christmas rush, washed dishes at Schrafft's, and worked as a bouncer at the famous Roseland ballroom. He had no way of knowing if this kind of life would continue until he became a middle-aged might-have-been. In retrospect, he says that at this point all he cared about was becoming a star. Unlike many actors, who say that making it is unimportant as long as they can work at their craft, Reynolds admits quite openly that it wasn't until later in his career that acting itself became as important to him as the trappings of being a star.

He fell in with a group of actors who taught him the ropes of survival in New York. He met them in a bar in Greenwich Village, where they passed the time between auditions and part-time jobs playing pool and exchanging advice and information. Being a struggling actor is about as insecure a position as anyone can be in, and the encouragement and support of peers is good medicine when the going is rough. When it isn't rough, it is always fun to swap stories. This hangout was one of the neighborhood spots that catered to young actors. It was their local watering hole, employment office, answering service, and second home. Burt studied the other young actors there the way he had studied Ned Davis.

One friend who helped him immensely in these early days was the then unknown Rip Torn, who was just starting out himself. Torn, a fellow Southerner, hailed from Texas and was as tough and masculine as Burt. He had learned to channel his tremendous drive and energy into acting, as Burt had his into football and would now seek to do in acting.

Torn also used up some of his vitality by playing basketball, and Burt soon played with him for the same reason. They were both bursting at the seams and needed the outlet that a good workout provides.

Rip had no compunction about expressing himself—sometimes to the chagrin of his new friend from Florida. Burt remembers: "We used to do voice exercises together. Once we were on the subway and Rip was doing his exercises (a series of snorts, shouts, and grunts) but I wasn't, so Rip yelled at me, 'You're never going to be

an actor because you're embarrassed.' Embarrassed? I still can't do that on the subway."

One day while he was at his hangout, Burt met someone from a locally produced show, *Frontiers of Faith*, who was looking for a young actor who could do what today would be done by stuntmen. In the days of live television, there was no such thing. Instead, they used actors who would say a couple of lines, get hit over the head, say a few more lines, get thrown out of a window, and after a few more, perhaps get tossed off a roof.

It may not have been *Hamlet*, but it was acting, and it paid a lot more than washing dishes. Burt's first part required him to get thrown through a window after saying his lines, and paid him $132 for a few hours' work. It was the first of a line of jobs in which he was punched in the jaw, pushed down flights of stairs, tossed out of windows, thrown off roofs, and bounced off walls. He had finally broken into the glamorous world of show business—the hard way.

With typical humor, Reynolds reflects that it was his days as a bouncer that gave him his first rudimentary lessons in being a stuntman. Watching patrons who had gotten out of line go whizzing down the stairs, and accidentally taking that route himself after a run-in with an unruly customer, Burt learned a lot about taking a professional nose dive!

These first jobs were better than taking unprofessional falls, but Burt wanted more. He decided to study acting. The Actors Studio was then the mecca for aspiring young actors, but Reynolds quickly decided it wasn't for him. "I saw seventeen Marlon Brandos, thirteen James Deans and fled. Strasberg was God then. It was the height of method acting. I don't think anyone learns in class. If they do, they fall apart onstage," Burt explained. He didn't believe that painfully exploring the soul was the way to become a good actor.

Two years and a lot of broken glass went by. Then, in 1957, Burt landed his first role on Broadway, moving up the ladder another rung. The play was a revival of the popular *Mr. Roberts*, starring Charleton Heston, and it opened at the prestigious City Center.

He might have moved up another rung soon afterward had it not been for a quirk of fate that would become a haunting refrain in Reynolds' career over the next decade.

He auditioned for a part in *Sayonara*, a movie being cast in New York. Although he did very well and everyone liked him, he didn't get the part. The reason? He looked too much like the movie's star, Marlon Brando.

It seemed bitterly ironic to lose a job because he looked too much like a movie star. What Burt didn't know then was that his resemblance to Brando would become

MCA

People who think of Burt as an overnight success don't realize that he put in fifteen years of hard work before anyone even heard of him.

The Silver Screen Archives

Burt got his first part on Broadway and hopes to return someday. Here he and friends are with the cast of *Annie*.

Burt put all the hard work into his movie career that he had put into his football career, and it paid off royally.

the bane of his existence. It was heartbreaking to lose one job after another because he looked too much like someone who had already made it into the limelight.

Now that Reynolds has lost weight and discarded his permanent scowl, there isn't that much of a resemblance, but twenty years ago, he says he looked more like Brando than Brando did. He weighed about two hundred pounds (twenty-five pounds more than today) wore the T-shirt-and-leather-jacket ensemble that Brando had made so popular, and had developed some of the sullen temperament to go with it. (It was an image he kept until his thirties, long after it had stopped being chic.) Being Brando's look-alike became a curse. Not only did it cost him several parts he would love to have played, but it also cost him more than one embarrassing moment.

One of these moments has become a favorite anecdote of Reynolds', but it was difficult to find it amusing at the time.

There's the classic story of the little old lady at the airport. "She came over and said she knew I was *Brando* and wanted my autograph. I said 'Lady, I'm not.' She

left to join her husband and then came back and said, 'My husband and I have talked it over and we know you're Marlon Brando.'

"I said in rather a loud voice, 'Damn it lady, I'm not Marlon Brando.' That was all she needed to be convinced. She said, 'Ah, now we *know* you're Marlon Brando.' "

Another incident was more embarrassing. A friend led him, unknowing, to a table where Brando himself was eating and pointed out the amazing resemblance. Brando merely rolled his eyes at the ceiling, rudely rebuffing Reynolds in front of the entire restaurant. Burt was so humiliated he took his date home and then drove to Brando's home, where he waited for four hours for the opportunity to have it out with him. Brando never came home.

Thoroughly discouraged, and with little hope that his prospects would get better, Burt decided to throw in the towel and go back to Florida. The image of sun-tanned coeds and applause from the bleachers became more alluring with each new acting rejection. He decided to return to college, go back to playing football, and look for a job as a football coach when he graduated.

It came as a rude awakening to find out that he wasn't able to play on the football field the way he'd thought he'd be able to. He'd thought his knee had sufficiently healed by this time and that he wouldn't have any problems with it, but that didn't turn out to be true. He was put on the second team, and even that he found challenging.

The moment of reckoning came when he made a fumble that cost his school the game. Even on the second team he couldn't make it! He felt like a complete failure. Then, suddenly, he knew that he was simply in the wrong ball park. Once again, he packed his clothes and left home, only this time he headed west. If you wanted to be a movie star, you went to Hollywood. Burt Reynolds wanted to be a star.

A strong resemblance to Marlon Brando caused Burt to lose many coveted movie parts when he was younger.

Burt played more cowboys and Indians in his early career than most actors play in a lifetime.

5/STRUGGLING FOR RECOGNITION

With the encouragement of his peers and teachers, a Broadway role under his belt, and the assurance that he was not only good-looking but talented—Burt Reynolds' success was fairly guaranteed. He arrived in Hollywood, took a screen test, was signed, and put on a conveyer belt to stardom.

Right? Hardly. Once in Hollywood, Reynolds began a long, hard climb. It took him fifteen years to see the top.

He was signed by a film company, but the conveyer belt he found himself on led to obscurity. He was on his way to becoming a well-known unknown, which in Hollywood is the kiss of death. He played so many insignificant roles as a succession of cops, robbers, cowboys, and Indians that his face became too familiar to raise any excitement from casting directors, and the parts he found himself in were nowhere good enough to gain him recognition as a star. "I was the only movie star who made it in spite of his pictures," he himself said wryly about that dismal period.

To say that he needed guts, stamina, and drive to keep plugging away when he was constantly relegated to second place in third-rate movies is an understatement. But Reynolds stayed in there, determined to hit pay dirt. He says that he always knew he would make it one day, and that he figured it would probably be when he was about thirty-five. He just didn't think he would make thirty-five, he adds with a grin.

The first obstacle he ran into when he reached Hollywood was a real Catch-22. The studios all required footage before they would even consider a new actor for a role—but it was impossible to get the footage until he had landed that all-important first part.

After being stopped dead in his tracks several times this way, Reynolds called home and asked his parents to send some 8-mm. film of him as a baby. The next time a casting director asked to see some film, that is what he showed him. The show they were casting for was *M Squad*, and the star was Lee Marvin, who appreciated

37

Burt has become the kind of movie star that Hollywood was full of in the days of John Wayne and Jimmy Stewart. Today, he and Clint Eastwood have cornered the market.

Reynolds' sense of humor and gave him his first part.

Hollywood was still being run with contract players in those days. It wasn't the way it had been in its golden era, when actors were groomed for stardom from their teen years on, but it wasn't the free-wheeling place it is today either. The usual course of events was for a young actor to be signed by a motion-picture company, which then went about the business of guiding him through the ranks.

Reynolds signed up with Universal, but it turned out to be a dead end. They slated him for the television series *Riverboat*, starring Darren McGavin. It was designed to give the popular *Maverick* on a competitive network a run for its money, but most of the running was done in circles. The show had problems from the begin-

Whether he's a cowboy or an Indian, Burt has an appeal that shines through.

For a long time, getting recognition seemed to be as hard as getting his characters out of trouble, but Burt managed to do both.

Pictorial Parade

Many people say they always knew he would be a star, but Burt says he himself didn't even know—he just hoped he'd make it by the time he was thirty-five.

ning, and Reynolds had more than his fair share of them.

His part was so small he often says the only thing he ever did as captain of the riverboat was occasionally blow the whistle; he thought of himself as "Dum-Dum the Whistle Blower." After he had been with the show for a while, the producers told him everything was going to change, that he would become the co-star and he and McGavin would alternate weeks as the leading man. It looked as though this might be the big break that Burt was expecting.

Unfortunately, things didn't work out that way. The tension between Burt and McGavin became unbearable. Burt's temper grew shorter by the day. Feeling completely frustrated and mistreated by the powers that be, one day he vented his wrath on the associate director with a punch in the jaw that sent him flying into the river.

He had taken all he could take. Not caring whether or not he was doing the

right thing for his career, he asked to be released from his contract. "They called me a lot of nasty names and said they'd put a shower in my dressing room and give me a better parking space on the lot and I said, 'You don't understand. I want OUT.' They called me some more names, but they let me out and they haven't been keen on me since," Reynolds remembers.

"Then I couldn't get a job. I didn't have a very good reputation; you don't just walk out on a network television series. I did some things like *Pony Express*, the kind of show they shoot with a Kodak and a flashlight. Those were depressing years."

If Reynolds had been frustrated on *Riverboat*, then he was really chafing at the bit now. He wanted to strut his stuff—show the world who he was and what he could do—but he was persona non grata in most television and movie casting offices.

In 1961, he decided to return to New York, where he landed a part in Hugh Wheeler's *Look, We've Come Through* on Broadway, directed by Jose Quintero. The professional experience was good, but he felt quite lost and lonely.

"I had a rough time on that. I was Mister Hollywood," he said, referring to the way people saw him. When the director started the day, he gave everyone a pat on the back except Reynolds. He was left to eat alone on the breaks. It was a very painful experience.

Burt received good reviews, which is a real tribute to his talent, since his part was very small. But nothing magical happened to send him rocketing to the top. Instead, he found himself in some easily forgotten films, including *Armored Command, Angel Baby,* and *Operation CIA.* "My movies were the kind they show in airplanes and prisons because nobody can leave," he quips today, from the vantage point of success.

In 1962, he was screened for the part of the half-breed in *Gunsmoke.* The initial exchange was not exactly friendly.

Riverboat, with Darren McGavin, was supposed to be Burt's first break, but it didn't work out that way.

"You're too fat in the face for an Indian," they told him. "If you want an Indian, go to Oklahoma. I'm an actor," he retorted. They must have liked his style, since they gave him the part—as Quint Asper, the blacksmith.

His two years on *Gunsmoke* were happy ones. It was a blockbuster show, and the success created a very convivial atmosphere on set. Burt made good friends, enjoyed himself immensely, made enough money to live like a movie star even if he wasn't one, and dated plenty of women. Then he met Judy Carne.

Burt is very protective toward the women in his life, and still holds to many values that are considered old-fashioned today.

6/JUDY CARNE

It was love at first sight. She thought he was handsome and witty. He thought she was funny and bright and a totally captivating free spirit. He was twenty-six and she was twenty-two. It was a powerful attraction and neither of them fought it. They lived together for a year, and got married. Then, three short years later, it was over, leaving them both with terrible pain and confusion.

When Burt Reynolds found himself attracted to Judy Carne, it came as a big surprise. His taste in women until then had been very different. He had dated a lot of women, from starlets to script girls, and most of them had been much more voluptuous than Judy Carne.

Then came Judy. He described her as a Peter Pan, elfin kind of creature, one of the original Flower Children. She was boyishly thin, perky, and childlike, but she had a mind of her own. She had been on her own since she had left her parents' home in Nottingham, England, at the age of sixteen. She was ambitious and somehow carefree at the same time. She had

the kind of sexiness that comes from tremendous vitality.

Most important of all for Burt, she had an abundant sense of humor, and she was the first woman who appreciated *his* wit and sense of the outrageous. She didn't think he was simply a gorgeous hunk of man (although, being human, she probably had no objections to his beautiful brown eyes and good build)—she thought he was one of the funniest men she had ever met. She also thought he was kind. She saw a side of him that had almost been lost in his effort to live up to an idealized image of himself.

From the time that Burt had started out in show business, he and everyone else cast him in the role of a virile, tough, macho man. He thought as long as he stood around with his "Number 3 Virile Look," he was doing what was expected of him. He came to believe in his own stereotype.

Judy saw beyond the male myth to the real man inside, and she loved what she saw. Burt responded to that love. He

Burt realized too late that he had very conservative ideas about marriage.

dropped the façade and felt free to relax and enjoy himself with her. He didn't have to try and impress her, he simply acted natural and found that by doing that, he did impress her.

Ironically, as much as Judy adored him, and though later she attested to his prowess in bed, she didn't think that the man who has since become the country's number-one sex symbol was sexy. She was drawn to him for many reasons, but that wasn't one of them. "I never thought of him as sexy," she stated later, "and I'm still surprised to hear him described as a sex symbol."

They lived together almost immediately after they met, and a year later got married. For a while, it was magical. They couldn't spend enough time together, talk enough, share enough, laugh enough.

They also couldn't spend enough. They both had modest backgrounds, so when they suddenly found themselves with money to burn, they did just that. Burt was making good money on a steady basis for the first time in his life on *Gunsmoke*, and Judy had a leading part in the popular situation comedy *A Fair Exchange*. It

seemed they had more money than Fort Knox.

They bought a big splashy house in Hollywood, which they proceeded to tear apart and put back together again. They brought in decorators and architects and contractors to create a dream house for themselves. Judy laughingly remembers that they monogrammed everything in sight. It was an exciting time for them both. They had everything they had ever dreamed of. It seemed as if they had found their happy ending.

Both had come from stable homes, were the children of parents who are to this day happily married to each other. Neither Burt nor Judy had entered into their marriage with the flighty attitude that characterizes so many Hollywood marriages— here today, gone tomorrow, "I'm gonna love you while I may." When they made their vows, it was for a lifetime. But when they said "for better or for worse," they had no idea what "worse" might entail.

The bubble burst all too soon. Burt decided there was room for only one leading man on *Gunsmoke*, and it definitely wasn't him. Hoping to further his career, he left the show and the security it represented.

Judy, later known as the "Sock It to Me Girl," was already the better known of the two. When they went places together, it was her autograph people wanted, her picture they took. This would be hard on any man, but for one who was struggling to make it in the same competitive business in which his wife was already succeeding, it was impossible. Burt's ego took a beating every time they stepped outside the door.

To make matters worse, Judy became the breadwinner of the family. Burt had quit with the idea of finding other work right away, but that didn't happen. Months went by, and nothing turned up for him. She was the one signing checks, the one with a job to fill her days, the one getting ahead in her career. It was a situation that the most mature and stable

Burt and "Sock It to Me" girl Judy Carne broke up because of money and career pressures that neither of them could handle.

The Silver Screen Archives

Burt was strongly attracted to elflike Judy, though she was very different from the voluptuous beauties he had been dating.

person would have difficulty with. For an insecure person, it was like living on top of dynamite with a chain smoker—and there is probably no such thing as a secure actor who is out of work. The main occupational hazard of actors is the harrowing difficulty of getting through periods of unemployment. It isn't just a matter of money; it is all the incumbent doubts, fears, and anxieties. Such times do not help a budding marriage to thrive.

Judy remembers those days with sadness. "I was earning $200,000 a year and Burt was earning very little. I was the breadwinner and it was very painful to Burt's ego to know that his wife was earning more money than he was. That's when things began to get rough," she said, explaining the beginning of the end of their marriage.

An additional element to this unhappy picture was that they had married with somewhat different expectations. Burt

loved Judy because she was a free spirit, but he didn't expect her to stay that way. He assumed that after they got married she would want to settle down, have children, and become a homemaker. He had very clear ideas concerning what married life should be like.

The trouble was, so did Judy. And they weren't the same ideas. She saw herself as being a Thoroughly Modern Married Lady. She had no intention of throwing her career aside to raise a family and be a full-time wife. She thought that their married life would be an extension of the way their lives had been when they lived together.

Burt later reflected on the irony that it was the very qualities that had drawn him to Judy that drove them apart. Her Tinker Bell love of freedom and unconventional ideas about how to live suddenly didn't seem so appealing to Burt. He realized, too late, that he had very conservative ideas about marriage that were formed by his own childhood and *Father Knows Best*. He didn't want a kookie marriage.

The tension became unbearable. Burt had more frustation and anger than ever building up inside him. Judy bought him a punching bag and hung it outside, to give him a way to vent his feelings. It didn't help.

Then, suddenly, Judy was out of work too, and the bills started pouring in. They had established a life style that was quite expensive to maintain, and there was no money in the coffer. They went deeply into debt, and the tension that had been mounting between them reached a breaking point.

"During one of our frequent fights, I told Burt I wanted out—a divorce—and in the heat of the argument he agreed," Judy said with surprise. "Before I knew it, we were no longer married." It all happened so quickly, there seemed to be no time to go back, no chance to make amends.

Looking back, Judy isn't sure that there

could have been any other outcome, considering the way they both were at the time and the strain their marriage was under. "We destroyed each other during our marriage. Burt and I are strong people, and our egos were just too big in those days and neither of us was willing to give," she said after their divorce.

Burt remembers their marriage with a lot of pain, but no regrets. "I never even looked at another chick when I was married to Judy," he stated. "When it was good with her, it was the best I ever had. But when it was bad, it was the worst," he said after they parted.

"I have no regrets—in fact, I'd go through it all again," he added.

The marriage was over; the pain and involvement lingered on. They avoided each other meticulously, unable to spend any time together at all. Long after the divorce papers were filed away, Burt admitted, "My heart beats faster when I hear her name."

Years went by before they were able to resume even a speaking relationship. Finally, in 1971, he had her on as a guest when he hosted *The Tonight Show*. The show received the highest ratings it had in years. Burt admitted to the press that in spite of their long separation, they spent the night together, and all the old electricity was there. However, a reunion was not on the books.

Though—or perhaps because—the spark was still there, they found it very uncomfortable to be together. Ignoring the past and all the heartache they had been through took too much out of them. Judy implied to the press that things were not completely over for them, and that that was the reason Burt avoided being alone with her.

"Burt's still afraid to be alone with me," she said. "When we do a show together, he makes sure there are plenty of people around. Even when we meet for lunch,

The divorce left Burt with a sense of failure and misgivings about marriage.

there is a third party," she said, referring in particular to a luncheon date when Burt was accompanied by Sarah Miles.

If Burt had any desire for a reconciliation, he kept it buried. Their divorce was a shattering experience, one he saw as a personal failure as well. To this day, he is gun-shy to the point of terror on the subject of marriage. The wounds ran deep. If they have healed, the scars certainly remain. He will have to be absolutely convinced it will work before he enters into marriage again.

At the time of his divorce, the possibility of another marriage later on was the last thing on Burt's mind. It felt as if he had come to the end of the line. Nothing was happening in his career, he felt like an outcast in his family, his marriage was over, he had serious money problems, and there were no solutions in sight. Little did he know that he was around the corner from having everything he had ever wanted—the love of a good woman, a reconciliation with his father, money galore, and the kinds of movie parts he had been waiting for.

Burt has had a hard time with the critics, but they seem to be coming around now. His fans have always been behind him though.

7/AQUARIAN MAN

To understand someone as complex and unusual as Burt Reynolds, it is helpful to take a look at his horoscope, for it tells a lot about him. Burt was born on February 11, 1936, which makes him an Aquarius with his moon in Libra.

Aquarius is the zaniest, most unpredictable, complex, independent, original, unconventional sign in the zodiac. To understand this sign is to realize that you can never completely understand anyone who was born under it, much less predict what he will do. An Aquarius has a mind of his own, and will always go his own way, no matter what the objections or obstacles. Then again, he may suddenly decide that that isn't the way he wants to go at all, and pursue a different path.

He is an original—a one-of-a-kind model. "When they made him, they broke the mold" was undoubtedly said of someone born under the sign of Aquarius.

There is no way to tie down an Aquarius. He is the original free spirit. Restrictions, rules, limitations of any kind simply aren't his style. He may stay put awhile, but only as long as he wants to, and then he is off again.

An Aquarius has his head in the clouds and his feet on the ground. An idealist and a romantic whose dreams are hanging on a moonbeam, he is also as pragmatic and realistic as the most hard-nosed lawyer. No matter how dreamy and fanciful he may be, underneath he always knows the score, and has probably arrived at it with a calculator.

Contradiction is his middle name. An Aquarius loves his fellow man, and is a friend to all, but he needs isolation and quiet solitude as much as he needs food and water. He may be surrounded by friends, of whom he is genuinely fond, but few of them will ever be close to him. It is very difficult to enter into the inner circle of anyone born under this sign. It is easy to be on jocular terms, but close friendship only happens after he has scrutinized you well. Once you have gained his trust, which is not an easy thing to accomplish, you have made a true friend for life, as anyone who is close to Reynolds can attest. He will go to any lengths for someone he considers a friend, and friendship is one of the most cherished things in his life.

While an Aquarius loves to experiment and be the first to try things, he doesn't expect everyone else to be the same way. He has a "live and let live" credo. He will always be the first one into the pool, but he will never push or even prod you to join him if you don't want to. As unconventional as he may be at times, he never tries to force his ideas on those around him. He is as accepting of other people as he is curious about how they came to be the way they are.

His interest in people is one of his charms. Until you realize that he is equally interested in everyone who comes his way, he makes you feel like the most fascinating person on earth.

His thirst for knowledge makes him want to know everything about everything from physics to philodendrons. He wants to explore and examine every part of life. Furthermore, he wants to experience it all. He isn't just inquisitive, content to sit home and read about the places he has never been. He wants to set precedents, go where angels fear to tread.

His curiosity makes him a veteran people-watcher (a hobby Reynolds has missed dearly since becoming so famous). The idiosyncrasies and motivations of people are his daily food for thought and rumination. This trait is invaluable to an actor, for it gives him a memory bank he can draw on in creating different roles.

Another Aquarian trait that is helpful to an actor is intuitiveness. Someone born under this sign has highly tuned antennae that pick up everything around him. He knows things that there is seemingly no way to know, simply because he feels them. This enables an actor like Reynolds to tune into a character he is going to portray, to "know" him on a gut level that

has nothing to do with rational thought processes. It also gives him the innate sensitivity to other people and their needs that has won Burt such loyal friends.

An Aquarius loves to be unfettered in any sense; unfailing individuality, and nudity are often associated with this sign. It came as no surprise to anyone who knew anything about astrology when Burt showed up, against the advice of friends and advisers, in the pages of *Cosmopolitan*, naked as the day he was born, and smiling with the satisfaction of knowing that once again he had broken all the rules. It was revealing in more ways than one.

Burt's sense of humor and timing, often based on the outrageous, are typical of this sign. Many of the best comedians we have had were Aquarians, including Jack Benny, Charlie Chaplin, George Burns, Jack Lemmon, Tommy Smothers, Ann Sothern, Jimmy Durante, and Joey Bishop.

Honesty is the hallmark of most Aquarians, and this trait is exhibited in Burt's personality time and time again. He has always been forthright, even when it would have behooved him to soften the truth a little. With women, in particular, he has always believed in telling the truth, even when it hurts—which it often does, since he has a well-known wandering eye and a voracious appetite for the opposite sex. Whereas most men would hedge and put up smoke screens to hide their extracurricular activities, Reynolds has always taken the hard line of the truth. This has undoubtedly placed him in some pretty uncomfortable spots, and been very painful for the leading lady in his life, but apparently the honesty pays off in the long run, since no one has left him for infidelity yet. It must be hard to stay angry at him for his indiscretions when he is so unfalteringly honest about them.

It is unusual, and not at all typical of his

sign, that Burt married at such a young age, for the average Aquarian stays away from marriage until he is well into middle age, if not senility. Perhaps this is the reason his marriage lasted such a short time. It may have been a simple case of having done something that was basically against his nature. His reluctance to tie the knot a second time is much more in line with his stars, making it unlikely that he will venture down the aisle again until there are a few more gray hairs on his head. Nothing ventured, nothing lost.

What was in keeping with his chart was his relationship with Dinah Shore. His Venus, the ruler of romance, is in Capricorn, which usually results in an attraction to someone older and more mature than the boyish Aquarian. The maturity and practical nature of Capricorn also helps to keep Burt's feet on the ground when his heart is taking flight. Capricorn is also known for its steadiness, which, combined with the Aquarian flightiness, may explain why Burt has always been a one-woman man who quite often has more than one woman. In view of his astrological chart, that doesn't seem to be so much a contradiction as an inevitability.

As well as being known for their zaniness, Aquarians often have mental capacities that place them in genius ranks. Combined with this superior intelligence are a lot of planetary signs of leadership. We may have only just begun to see what Reynolds is capable of, especially in the field of directing, which would be a natural for him. When he really breaks out and applies himself in this area, he may discard his acting career entirely and become one of the giants in the film industry as a director.

Burt always has time for his fans—especially when they're pretty women.

Hamilton/Globe Photos

Burt says he doesn't even know most of the women his name has been romantically linked to in the gossip columns.

8/BURT'S KIND OF WOMAN

So many women, so little time. The way most reporters tell it, this is Reynolds' theme song, sung by a Lothario who litters the world with broken hearts. He is the Playboy of the Western World, lusting after every new lovely who crosses his path.

Not so, says Reynolds. He has an obvious and enthusiastic liking for women, but he isn't a Don Juan. In fact, he says with a mischievous grin, he's glad that people write about the many women he goes out with, because it gives him a chance to actually meet some of them. The fact is, he doesn't even know many of the women his name has been linked with.

It is also a fact that Reynolds is rarely seen with the kind of glamour girls other men in his position might be drawn to, the kind he himself favored in his earlier days. None of the women he has dated seriously have been the big-breasted, low-cut, sparkly type. The woman he married looks more like Peter Pan than most twelve-year-old girls. He himself describes Dinah Shore as "chicken soup,"

which seems apt. She is a beautiful, charming, and accomplished woman, but there is nothing flashy about her. She is . . . well, chicken soup. Chrissie Evert, whom many people predicted would be *the* girl, is obviously more at home in the great outdoors than she is in a nightclub, and more comfortable in shorts than in something slinky. And Sally Field, his constant companion and rumored wife-to-be, is pert and sexy, but hardly a *femme fatale*.

Burt is drawn to women who are real, wholesome, intelligent, and most of all, have a good sense of humor. He likes a woman who is unaffected and likes to have fun. Just as he doesn't spend his free time hanging out with the jet set, he isn't turned on by racy women—at least not for long-term relationships. He isn't looking for someone out of the pages of *Vogue*—he prefers a woman who will jump on the back of his motorcycle and not worry about messing up her hair, someone who will be happier watching old movies on TV and making popcorn than going to a

Gossip columns link Burt's name with every leading lady he does a movie with, but he says the stories just aren't true. The leading lady here is Cybill Shepherd.

Hollywood premiere.

At times Reynolds may be unimpressed by a woman's beauty, but the one thing that knocks him out every time is a good sense of humor. It is the most appealing quality a woman can have, as far as he is concerned. Naturally, he appreciates a pretty face, but after working with some of the world's great beauties—Lauren Hutton, Cybill Shepherd, Raquel Welch, Candice Bergen, and Catherine Deneuve, to name a few—the thrill is gone. He can appreciate a woman's looks, but when it comes to spending time with her, he wants someone with personality. With that well-known self-mocking humor, he explains that he loves to laugh in bed—and adds that sometimes the extra time comes in handy.

He is drawn to a lady who has many facets to her personality, the kind of woman who is hard to define. He likes a woman to be totally self-sufficient, and yet says he is something of a chauvinist, definitely preferring to be in charge of the situation. He likes to have a raucously good time, and he also likes to spend quiet evenings reading poetry by the fire. He wants a woman who will be completely devoted to him, and yet he wants her to be her own person, and likes it if she gives him a run for his money. He often says he doesn't want to be tied down—and just as often he says that he wants to settle down and have a family.

One of the reasons Burt is so appealing to women is that he honestly *likes* them. As most women know all too well, this isn't true of a lot of men. Many men would rather spend time around the pool table joking about sex and "trading lies" than actually doing anything about it.

Reynolds, on the other hand, genuinely likes spending time with women—from little girls to little old ladies. When he says that some of his best friends are women, it sounds like a good line for an interview, but it happens to be true. He is sincerely fond of the women in his life, and has remained good friends with almost every one he has ever been involved with.

Most women instinctively know this, whether they have actually met him or have simply seen him on a talk show. They sense his vulnerability and his genuine liking for them, and they respond to it. And, of course, they also instinctively sense his ability as a lover. It seems that if his reputation as a Don Juan is not deserved, his reputation as a lover *is*.

Ex-wife Judy Carne says that this is because he is a giver. The thing that gives him the most enjoyment in sex is *giving* enjoyment. This is a truly rare quality, and one that any woman worth her salt recognizes intuitively. It is no wonder that Reynolds has become such a popular sex symbol. As well as being good-looking and funny, he exudes the feeling that he is one of the world's all-time great lovers.

Ironically, his "macho" reputation really has nothing to do with his sexual appeal. That appeal comes from the impression that he is in tune with women and their needs.

"The idea of masculinity and virility is changing around completely. The guy I played in *Deliverance* was real macho," he explains. "He'd think you were a homosexual if you didn't have a gun rack in your house. But women don't care about ducks and bears all over the walls. Weight lifting is narcissistic, it's for the man himself, to impress other men. I know. I used to go in for that," he says,

Lauren Hutton was another leading lady whom the fan magazines tried to link with Burt.

For a while, it was rumored that Burt and Liza were a hot item, but it turned out to be untrue.

referring to his earlier years. "I used to think weight lifting was the greatest thing in the world."

He has also said of Lewis, the character he played in *Deliverance*, that the excitement that Lewis got from killing a man in the act of saving another was orgasmic, and that he consciously played it that way. He also found something essentially homosexual in his relationship with the character played by Jon Voight, which is an interesting observation on macho men.

The understanding Burt has of the complex world of sex and romance comes from much experience and reflection. One of the conclusions he has reached is that the real excitement for him comes in the mystery and the ambience, not the conquest. This is one of the things that makes him a true romantic.

He thinks that "sublety in romance is more important than just jumping in and out of bed.

"Flirting is the great thing. It never went out of style. Anticipation of the final event is often more fun than the actual conquest. Just as in the movies, it's not the final fight, but the buildup that's exciting."

His romanticism is also revealed in one of his favorite anecdotes—a story of the mystery and excitement of a fleeting moment.

It happened at a party. Across the room, his eyes met those of a beautiful woman. Although the electricity hummed between them, he didn't meet her until after the party, and then for only a few seconds. He says that they never touched, and knew that they would never meet again, but that it was one of the most exciting and romantic moments of his life.

Reynolds *has* lived out some of his favorite fantasies.

"I was on a cruise once, and you can't be on a ship without falling in love at least once," he said about one such incident. "There was this doll by the pool and she was devastating. I had just seen 427 guys get shot down and I knew whatever line I delivered it would have to be good.

"I thought about it while a few more guys got shot down, then I went up to her and said, 'I don't really have a line. I just want to jump your bones.' It worked. Three days later I reeled out of her cabin," he said with a smile that went from ear to ear.

Another incident took place while he was on location down South. He had given an interview saying that his idea of the perfect woman was a unique combination of courtesan and lady. One night there was a knock on his trailer door, and when he opened it, a lovely woman looked at him, pointed to the magazine article in her hand, and said she was that woman. She stayed with him for the duration of the film, and they are still good friends today.

It is typical of the kind of thing that happens to Reynolds. He gets everything from overt photographs to lacey valentines in the mail. He has been approached in person with every conceivable kind of proposition from demure to basic. One time while he was eating in a restaurant in Florida, the waitress leaned over and whispered to him, "Wanna hump?"

One woman's ardor was so great, her husband offered to pay Burt $800 to have drinks with his wife and kiss her. He kissed her three times, got "smashed" with them, and gave the money to charity.

Not all men are so understanding about the passion Reynolds inspires in their mates. He has been accosted more than once by an angry spouse who caught his wife making eyes at him across the room.

He has also had his share of hostile women who have approached him with the "So, you think you're pretty good in the sack—eh?" taunt. He doesn't let it bother him. Why should he? He knows who he is.

The only thing that seems to bother him is rudeness in a woman's advances. He doesn't understand why a phone call making a proposition to him has to be made at three in the morning, and he considers that kind of timing poor manners.

On the other hand, among his favorite approaches are the innocent ones that come from young girls. He received one tribute that extolled his virtues in rhyme, included a fan to keep him cool in the heat, and said that the sender was available to operate it. He loved it.

The fact that in this day and age, women feel free to make the first move is something that Reynolds thinks is terrific. He has no quarrel with women's lib in that department.

"It's wonderful that a lady can sit at a bar alone nowadays and meet a man, leave with him, and acquire a friend instead of a reputation," he says. He isn't too comfortable with a girl completely taking over the male role, though. If he takes a woman out and she ends the evening by saying "It was nice, I'll call you," he is less than enthused.

"She'll call me? That's hard for a guy like me to take," he exclaims.

There are a few other things he finds difficult to accept in a female. One is a woman who swears a lot. Another is a swinger mentality. He is also put off by "hip" jargon. He runs in the other direction if a girl dots her conversation with "heavy," "right on," and "far out," just as he is left cold by the kind of trite and brainless approach like "What are your hobbies?" Basically he is also offended by a woman who is too cheap or doesn't give some care and thought to the way she presents herself.

Burt Reynolds does demand a lot from a woman if he is going to invest his time and interest in her. She has to be sophisticated enough to carry on an interesting conversation, yet exuberant enough to join him in his outdoor activities as well as his indoor ones. She has to stand on her own two feet, but be careful not to step on his toes. She can be outrageous, if she can carry it off, but he wants her to be soft and feminine as well.

Photoreporters

Lorna Luft was a constant companion for a while.

The women who have gone out with Reynolds are too numerous to mention in this book. He may say he isn't a womanizer, but he is a normal male who has spent most of his life as a single man around some of the most desirable women in the world, so naturally he has had more than his share of experience.

"I always seem to come off like Henry VIII rather than a guy who's just healthy, unattached, and trying to have a good time," he complains.

When it comes to long-term relationships, however, Burt hasn't had an outrageous number. On the contrary, he has had a few very fulfilling relationships with women who speak very highly of him and maintain friendships with him still.

Aside from Dinah, Judy, and Sally—certainly the most serious of his romances—the other women of import in his life have been Tammy Wynette, Chris Evert, Lorna Luft, and Miko Mayama. An interesting observation is that not one of them is alike in terms of looks, age, or temperament. Each is unique and special to Burt for very different reasons.

Very little is known about any of his relationships, and that is because he is very protective toward the women in his life. He has an old-fashioned gallantry that prevents him from talking to the press about anyone he is seeing—even when it would be to his benefit to do so.

A lifelong friend of his explained this. "Burt would rather have the devotion and appreciation of even one lady that he's been involved with than any sort of image the public might conjure up. What I'm saying is, Burt would rather seem like a heel to 200 million people and appear to be a hero to one girl he's known and loved—even for a very short time. He's really a very warm, humble kind of guy. Personally, I think he's very old-fashioned. I really do think he still believes in a lady's honor and I think he'd sink his whole reputation rather than besmirch one girl's name."

Nonetheless, he likes a very modern forthrightness in a woman. He has always been very honest and outspoken himself, and he respects a lady who is the same way. "I'm attracted to gutsy women," he explains. "I like women who'll come right out and say 'I like you'—it takes courage to say that—instead of saying 'I like your work, your acting, your clothes, your car.' What does that mean? I like a woman who can come right out and say it and not be embarrassed by it. But there's a paradox here, because I don't like women to be too demonstrative. The woman who crawls all over you in front of a lot of people is going to be all tired out by the time you take her home. I can't handle that either."

While he may like being a sex symbol professionally, personally it seems to embarrass him, which is why he constantly makes fun of himself and his image.

"I mock my own image, you know, the whole male sex symbol thing," he says. "I try to blow it right out of the water. But it seems the more you send it up, the more people take it the other way.

"They put you on the cover of *Time* magazine and call you a honcho macho—whatever the hell that is. When you read something like that, it sounds like you studied elocution with Charles Bronson."

Sometimes, when he tries to make fun of the picture everyone has of him as a stud, it backfires. When one reporter asked him why he has mirrors on his bedroom ceiling, he told him that when he woke up in the morning, he wanted to be able to see the person he loved most in the world. Everyone took the remark so seriously that he was very embarrassed, especially since he had thought it was obvious he was kidding. (When he was asked the same question on the *Merv Griffin Show*, he replied that it was to make the room look bigger—then made a Groucho Marx face and said if Merv believed that, he had some swamp land he'd like to sell him.)

In appearances on talk shows he demonstrates the kind of easygoing charm he has with women. When he takes questions from the audience, he flirts, flatters, cajoles, and charms every woman he talks to, making every one of them, no matter how plain or old, feel like a million dollars.

As with the sex symbol of all time, Clark Gable, an interesting paradox arises from Burt's fondness for women. He is a one-woman man, but he also likes to play the field. He likes the security and solidity of a relationship with one person, and he gives a lot to that woman. But he also has a roving eye, and sometimes the rest of him isn't far behind. Many of the stories about his meanderings are simply concoctions of the press, but then again, some are true.

It takes a very special kind of woman to be able to accept this. He has said quite openly that "I don't lie to women, but I do fool around." He seems to want to make it clear that, ultimately, there are no strings on him, and that forewarned is forearmed.

When it comes to marriage, Reynolds has opinions that come and go with the tides. Sometimes he has been quoted as saying that he will get married as soon as he finds the right woman, because the one thing he really wants out of life is to settle down and have a family.

More frequently, when the question of matrimony comes up, Burt is quick to reply with a quip. One time he said he belonged to "Marriage Anonymous," and that every time he felt the urge to get married coming on him, he called another member to avert the disaster.

Another time, when a reporter asked him if he believed in marriage, he answered, "Sure, I believe in good marriages. I also believe in the tooth fairy."

When he was seeing Dinah, he said that he seriously doubted he would ever marry again, and that, furthermore, he was not encouraged by the marriages he saw around him.

"My instinct right now is that I don't think I will ever get married again. In every business—not just the entertainment field—I see terrible marriages. Whenever I see a good one, I want to take it and just put it under a microscope and look at it.

"I'm not cynical about marriage," he continued. "I get knocked out about somebody and I think, 'She has all the qualities I've been looking for.' But I know how dreams sometimes vanish when you're actually married." Then, seeming to discount everything he had just said, he added, "I'm too big a romanticist to give up on everything entirely."

Since his relationship with Sally Field has solidified, he has expressed interest more and more often in marrying again. He may have finally found a woman to whom he can make that commitment.

Miko Mayama was one of the first girl friends Burt was really serious about.

Phototrends

Burt thinks his reputation as a "Macho Man" is amusing. He loves Zen poetry and talking quietly by a fire.

9/THE MACHO IMAGE MELLOWS

When he divorced Judy, it was a very serious matter to Burt. No one in his family had ever gotten a divorce. He felt the disappointment and failure bitterly.

It wasn't just the end of his marriage. Suddenly, he saw his entire life in terms of quitting. He felt like a failure in everything. Nothing in his life made any sense.

He called home and told his mother that his father had been right about him all along: he was a quitter. He had quit college, quit football, quit his television jobs, and now he had quit his marriage.

He didn't know that his father was listening on the other line. Burt Sr. interrupted the conversation and told his son to come home.

The plane ride home was a long one. Visions of his life flashed before Burt's eyes, and they all seemed outlined in disappointment and failure. He had no idea how his father would greet him, what he would say.

When he got home, he and his father went out into the backyard with a bottle of cognac. They talked into the night, shar-ing thoughts and hopes and broken dreams. When they had finished, they were close in a way they had never been before, and it literally marked a new beginning for Reynolds in almost every way.

There is a saying in the South that "No man is a man until his father tells him he is." Reynolds is fond of quoting this, and saying that if that night had been different, and his father had castigated him instead of giving him love and support, he might still be fighting the world and himself today.

Until that night, Burt had always loved his father, but it was the kind of love that is founded on respect and fear. He wasn't close to him, and never knew him as a man. He described him as "the kind of man who filled doorways." All the stories he told about his father pictured him as an almost legendary hero. One was about the time a man offered him $15,000 in a paper bag as a bribe when he was a sheriff, and he made the man eat the bag. Another was about the time he stopped a barroom fight by walking up to a man with a gun and taking it calmly out of his hand. The gun was cocked, loaded, and pointed at him when he did it.

Burt held his father in tremendous esteem, and didn't feel that his father approved of him at all. The night he returned home, he kept expecting his father to tell him he was a loser and a wastrel. When, instead, his father was understanding and shared with him all the mistakes he himself had made, a major change took place inside Burt.

He began to cry, and for the first time in his life he felt that it was all right to show emotion. All the ideas he had held all his life about being a "real" man and being strong and not showing feelings disappeared. He and his father embraced, and Burt told him that from then on, he was going to hug him like that every time he saw him. He says that now, when they

Burt hopes that he has seen the last of his cowboy/macho movies. He wants to make light romantic comedies like the ones that made Cary Grant famous.

The Silver Screen Archives

greet each other in airports, they are almost embarrassingly affectionate.

Once he knew that his father loved and accepted him, Burt lost the need to bash his head against the wall looking for love and acceptance everywhere else. Having gotten it from his father, he no longer needed to look for it in other people. Most of all, the reconciliation enabled him to accept himself. "All I ever wanted was to be popular," he explains today.

This reunion turned out to be a lifesaver for Burt. It marked the beginning of a whole new attitude toward life. The resentful, rebellious, angry young man began to grow up.

After that, a lot of things began to change for Burt. In 1966, he finally became the star of his own television series, *Hawk*. Located in New York City, it was something like an updated *Naked City*, with plenty of fast-moving, hard-punching action, centered around Detective Hawk, an angry part-Indian city cop.

He may have been cast as an Indian again, but this time he had a chance to do some good acting in a show that was well put together—and one that gave him a starring role for the first time. It may not have been everything he was looking for, but in many ways it was his first big break.

The idea of playing on television an Indian "who didn't talk gibberish or get plastered appealed to me, but it was a constant fight," he said about the show.

"If they had their way, I'd have been running around in moccasins and feathers. In the pilot film, they gave me knives to have up my sleeves but I refused to go along with it.

"I felt Bill Cosby had done much for the Negro on TV by playing a detective without racial reference. I wanted to play an American Indian in the same way," he explained.

It was a show with a lot of action, and gave Burt the chance to stage a lot of "gags," as stuntmen call their dangerous

Sam Whiskey was a real sleeper of a movie—still not well known, but one of Burt's favorites.

feats. "Hawk needs physical contact. He has the physical drive—you see that he has to hold back to keep from shoving somebody out a window.

"Not that he's trying to lick the world, and neither am I, anymore. I've found you can't take on the whole world in this business. But I'm happy here as an actor, I'm learning, I'm doing, I'm in every scene, I'm working with wonderful groovy New York actors, and I think it's going to be a habit-forming show."

It admittedly felt good finally to be the bride instead of the bridesmaid. "Having been in two TV series—*Gunsmoke* and *Riverboat*—where I held the horses for somebody else, this feels great," he said with obvious pleasure.

Many very anxious moments happened on the set as the result of the series being shot in one of the most colorful cities in the world, and Reynolds enjoyed them all immensely.

"In one instance we were shooting on a bridge and the police were in a desperate gunfight. A woman motorist drove right up to one of the officers crouching with gun in hand and asked him for directions to Ellis Island.

"In a scene on Broadway, the street had been roped off and the body of a supposedly dead man lay there. A middle-aged woman, somewhat inebriated, walked onto the scene, clutched the body in remorse and moaned, "Oh, you poor man!" It took a bit of a struggle to free her from the corpse."

All in all, it was the best experience Reynolds ever had. "Thinking back," he says, "I see that *Hawk* was the happiest year of my life in this business," he said after it was canceled. "For the first time, I didn't feel like a chess pawn. I helped direct, cast, write scripts, and fought the establishment, i.e., ABC–Screen Gems.

"I fell in love with that side of the business and realized directing is really what I'm aiming for. Since then I've done a couple of $4–$5 million movies but have not been as happy as with that dumb little series."

The critics thought Reynolds and the show were great, but unfortunately that wasn't enough to keep the series on the air. The cutthroat numbers game of network television killed it. It was in a time slot that pitted it against multimillion-dollar extravaganza movies and it didn't have a chance. Instead of moving it to another time period, the network canceled it, and Burt was out in the cold again.

He had been riding high, and now, once more, he had a handful of good reviews and a mouthful of dust. This time, it was especially hard because he had put so much of himself into the series, and the cancellation had seemed so premature and unnecessary.

He swore he'd never be in another television show, convinced that for him it was a road that led to nowhere. Time passed. He got parts in *Navajo Joe* in 1967, in *Shark*, *Impasse*, and *Fade In* in 1968, in *Sam Whiskey* and *100 Rifles* in 1969, and in *Skullduggery* in 1970. In other words, nothing much happened for him.

Most of the films were low budget, and most of the parts he played were Indians, which he didn't find amusing. "The scripts for a lot of the early films I did get were Steve McQueen or Robert Redford rejects . . . and they were right about 'em. Mainly, though, my big mistake was admitting I'm one-fourth Indian. When the studios spotted that in my talent profile, it was largely Indian roles for me for the next ten years. In the *Hawk* series on TV, I was described as 'a detective of American Indian descent who puts his natural instincts to use tracking down criminals.' How about that? I'm much closer to Italian ancestry. Maybe if they'd made the series about a pizza parlor, it would have lasted longer."

He didn't seem to be getting anywhere except from one forgettable film to another, so when he was offered the leading role in Quinn Martin's new series *Dan August*, he changed his mind about not being on television again. Martin had an excellent reputation for putting together a good show, and it didn't seem that Burt had much to lose by trying.

It was another tough-guy cop role, but at least it kept Burt in the public eye as a masculine, sexy actor. It still wasn't getting him where he wanted to go, though, and he had reached the magic thirty-five, the age he had designated as the time that everything would come together for him. He didn't know it yet, but he was right.

This show got canceled too, but this time Burt didn't feel as angry as he had about *Hawk*. He understood the reasons, and felt that they had at least given it a fair try this time. "I wish the show would go on," he said, "but I really don't see a chance. It is a very expensive show to produce, ratings are not great . . . and there are panic-button pushers.

"We were spending about $300,000 an episode and that is a pile of money. I am not ashamed of the product."

He knew his career was, or could be, at a major crossroad. He took a terrific chance. He went on national television and made fun of himself and everything he had done.

He started by announcing the cancellation of his show on the *Merv Griffin Show*, saying that he thought it was great that he was the only actor he knew who had the distinction of being in shows canceled by all three networks.

He talked about what turkeys his pictures were, slamming himself and all his movies with ruthless Don Rickles-type lines. The big difference is that Don Rickles isn't a leading man. No one in Burt's position had ever done what he proceeded to do. He not only made outrageous fun of himself, he completely

was drawing to an end. He cast Best as the villain.

Subsequently Reynolds cast Best in *Gator*, *The End*, and *Hooper*. Since Best is a very talented and experienced actor, Reynolds hadn't hired him just from a sense of obligation, but it is typical of Reynolds to choose a friend for a picture if he can. In fact, any picture in which he has had any say in the casting and crew abounds with friends and past acquaintances.

Another typical story is that when Burt learned he was going to direct *Gator*, he stopped by to visit his old friend Watson Duncan in Palm Beach. He asked him and his wife, Honey, who had done some local theater work, if they would like to be in the movie. "We thought he was kidding when he asked us to be in it," Duncan exclaimed. "We were absolutely beside ourselves."

"It was very exciting, and he was so wonderful to us. He treated us as though we were stars. He gave us everything—a chauffeur at our disposal, the whole treatment. He even put our names and a star on the dressing room door."

One thing in particular that Reynolds did moved Duncan tremendously. "When he was working on one scene that my wife was in, he suddenly called my name over the loudspeaker. When I came running in, he said, 'Look through the camera at your wife. She's absolutely beautiful!'

"He stopped the entire production so I could do that! Who in the world would do something that thoughtful? It touched me so much I almost cried."

Burt has said many times that his friendships are the most important thing in his life. He works hard at those friendships, as anyone must who takes his relationships seriously. He knocks himself out to do things for his friends, to make sure they are all right—ultimately, because that makes *him* happy. It is no wonder he is so well loved.

Burt looks great in a tuxedo, but is happier in jeans and a T-shirt.

In many of his movies, Burt was the only one who emerged with good reviews. *At Long Last Love* was one—the movie bombed, but everyone said that Burt was terrific as a song-and-dance man.

14/SUPERSTARDOM AT LAST

If the talk shows established Reynolds as a celebrity, and the *Cosmo* centerfold established him as a sex symbol, certainly *Deliverance* established him, finally, as an actor.

Based on the best-selling novel by James Dickey, this film is a classic, the kind of film that any actor would be proud to be in. It illuminates the nature of man and life, using an action-adventure format to make its point about man and how he goes about the matter of survival. Directed by John Boorman and also starring Jon Voight, this film gave Reynolds the opportunity to do some strenuous acting.

He played the part of Lewis, a "man's man" who lived to pit himself against nature and come out the survivor.

"It was probably the toughest acting job I ever had," he exclaimed. "I may be a lot of things, but macho to me is something you make fun of, and I've always had a self-deprecating sense of humor about the whole image, which is the whole reason for the *Cosmopolitan* thing."

The irony is that many people mistook the character in *Deliverance* for Reynolds' own, thus denigrating his talent as an actor. Burt says, "I still have the *New York Times* review of that picture. It was a Sunday piece about how brilliantly John Boorman had used this dumb macho guy to play this dumb macho guy."

This kind of critical put down was common enough when Burt's career began to soar, and it was painful to him.

Reynolds did all his own stunt work in the film including some very dangerous sequences in which he almost drowned two or three times. In one scene going down the rapids, they had planned to use a mannequin because it was so perilous. But each time the boat came down the river, it broke into splinters against the rocks and the dummy bounced all over and looked very obvious, so Reynolds decided to do it himself. Being a born adventurer, he loved every minute of the danger. "It's a terribly sensual feeling to go down a river at fifty miles per hour," he said with gusto.

But most of the exhilaration came from

Burt makes his acceptance speech after being given a star in the sidewalk along Hollywood Boulevard.

being thrown into a really demanding acting situation, putting everything he had into it, and ending up with a quality film. He unequivocally stated that it was "the best film I've ever been in. A classic of its kind. The kind of *Wages of Fear* picture that just picks you up and crashes you against the rocks. You feel everything and just crawl out of the theater. It was beautifully cast and fabulously directed. . . . it happens to be Stanley Kubrick's favorite film. He's seen it twenty-five times. He still says, 'Those were the real actors; how did you get those shots?' Well, how we got those shots was we just did it. There were very few actors who would've done that. We were all a little crazy then. And Vilmos Zsigmond (the cameraman) was right there in the middle of the river with us. As was John Boorman. We shot it with just sixteen men. We just did it. It was my deliverance out of bad films," he said.

"That was the turning point of my career," Burt said about the importance of this film to him. "After *Deliverance*, I considered myself an actor. A lot of people still don't believe it, but I do. *Deliverance* was an ensemble work. We lived those parts. The picture was shot in sequence,

from front to back, and you can see it if you just notice how we improve in handling the canoes as the film progresses."

Unlike the *New York Times* article that Reynolds still has stashed away, most of the reviews of the film and Reynolds himself were stunning. Many agree with his contention that if he hadn't appeared in the pages of *Cosmopolitan*, he might well have won an Oscar for his powerful performance.

The year 1972 marked the beginning of a four-year period that was a good one for Burt. He had his failures (although by now a failure for him was something that fell short of a box-office smash) but he was busy, and did some films that secured his place as one of the country's leading movie idols. In *Everything You Always Wanted to Know About Sex* he was in a cameo role, but it was completely removed from anything he had ever done before. *Shamus, Fuzz, The Man Who Loved Cat Dancing*, and *White Lightning* drew on his skills as a physical actor and leading man who had both humor and sex appeal.

The Longest Yard gave him a chance to return for a while to his original love, football. Robert Aldrich's film is about an ex-pro ball player who gets thrown in prison for stealing his Sugar Mama's sports car and dumping it in the river for spite. The most important thing in the warden's life is the football games between the prison inmates and guards, and he pressures Reynolds into coaching the prisoners' team—well, but not so well that they can win. What results is a gem of a film about underdogs.

This film is particularly important in Reynolds' career because it marks his complete transformation into a "Movie Star." When it was released, it was advertised as a prison movie. They couldn't give the tickets away. Then the marketing men changed the campaign and advertised it as a football film (forty minutes of the movie was, indeed, an actual football

Gator McCluskey, first seen in *White Lightning,* and here in *Gator,* is one of Burt's most popular characters.

game). Still nothing. Then they changed tactics again and billed it as a "Burt Reynolds movie," picturing him in a football outfit that looked painted on. Ticket lines went around the block and *The Longest Yard* became one of Reynolds' biggest box-office successes. He had definitely arrived.

Next he played more "good ol' boy" parts, and then went out on a limb by singing and dancing his way through *At Long Last Love.* The movie bombed but Reynolds garnered some praise for his scrapbook. In 1976, he took another giant step forward, this time into the field of directing. The movie was *Gator,* which recounted the continuing perils and adventures of Gator McCluskey, the ex-con and moonshiner who had won people's hearts in *White Lightning.*

In his inimitable style, Burt said they hadn't given him much to work with, but that he did the best he could to make chicken salad out of chicken shit. The movie had the expected quota of car chases, boat races, bawdy humor, and fast action, and featured some good performances by Lauren Hutton, Jack Weston, Jerry Reed, and of course, Burt himself.

As Reynolds' cult of diehard fans grew, so did his clipping book of reviews. More and more of the critics were realizing that he was indeed a good actor, though some persisted in doing a hatchet job on both him and his movies. Understandably, it hurt. He had spent so many years being frustrated that he wasn't allowed to act, it seemed to him bitterly unfair that now that he was doing some things he was proud of, certain critics refused to see it. "I spent a long time playing the third Indian from the left, and all the time I knew that I'd be best in things that weren't serious. I think I can play Burt Reynolds better than anyone in town, but then they say I'm not trying. It's hard to make acting look easy. There are two or three young actors around—I won't mention any names—who if I see them painfully staring at the rug in one more picture, I'm gonna puke.

"But when I'm in a halfway successful movie, it irritates the hell out of the critics in New York, because they'd like to kill my pictures if they could. So maybe I'm pretty good in a movie. Then they use all these words like I'm 'surprisingly' good, or 'shockingly enough,' I'm good. It's like I crawled out from under a magazine and they're surprised I can act," he said, angrily puffing on a thin black cigar.

"The other day I had a meeting with the studio. I said I had nothing against making this kind of movie that people expect to see me in," he said, referring to *Gator*

and all his other "Burt Reynolds movies," "but please don't put out an ad campaign where they take my shirt off and chisel me to the side of a mountain with six people clinging to my legs. This is a picture I'd like to see cross the Mason-Dixon line."

Though some critics continued to mock him snidely every time he did take his shirt off, he found it increasingly easy to ignore them and go his own way as his strength and stature as a star increased. By the time he made *Smokey and the Bandit*, he could howl all the way to the bank. The movie has a permanent place in theaters in the South, a semipermanent place up North, and is on its way to making a cool $200 million.

Smokey is quintessential Reynolds. It has everything that his fans love him for—

Many of the feelings that Sonny had in *The End* were like the ones Burt had when he was very ill and didn't know what was wrong.

lots of laughs, action-packed fun, and just enough sexiness. Much of the film seems real because there was so much spontaneity in the shooting of it, with all the actors letting loose and having a good time with the script.

Once again, Reynolds had won by following his instincts and doing something against the advice of those in the know. "Of course I was encouraged by the success of *Smokey*. Everybody had urged me not to do it. But I knew it would only take six weeks and I'd hardly have to get out of the car, so I saw no big problem. And I rewrote everything. I ad-libbed almost every line I had in the picture. So did Jackie Gleason. He never said one word the way it was written. So the whole thing had an improvisational feeling to it."

He also got consistently good reviews for the first time. "I don't understand it," he said, revealing how much the criticism had hurt. "I'm starting to get notices. Do you suppose the critics all got together in a room somewhere and said, 'Listen, let's stop kicking the daylights out of Reynolds; he's never going to give up?'"

The attitude that some critics had toward Reynolds rubbed off on many people who read them. "Kirk Douglas told me he saw that film five times," Burt said of *Smokey*. "And he didn't apologize, like most people do. Most people say, 'I didn't want to go, but the kids made me. And do you know something? I actually enjoyed it.' Usually I just say something like 'Too bad.'

"I don't know where that patronizing attitude comes from. Maybe from that centerfold business. Maybe from my early work. I'm the first to admit that when I look at my early TV it's just awful. I see no potential at all in myself, just a guy glaring around, dark and brooding. But I've grown since then, and it's taken a long time for the critics to realize that. I've grown because I'm not afraid of making a

Burt hopes to direct more movies, and people who have worked with him predict he will be one of the most important directors someday.

fool of myself. Today I look at the camera as someone I've been having an affair with for the past twenty years and who's only just realized how good in bed I am."

After *Smokey*, one thing was certain: no one could dispute Burt Reynolds' box-office strength. But he was still stifled by his own success. He wanted to do a movie like *Magic* or *All the President's Men* or *California Suite*, but the only scripts he got were postmarked from Redneck Country.

"It's the studios," he explained, complaining about the way he had. been trapped by typecasting. "If I had played a pink flamingo and it made lots of money, you'd be amazed at how many pink-flamingo parts would suddenly appear on my desk. They'd just start pasting feathers on me and I'd be dancing up and down the street. I'd be the 'Pink Flamingo in Paris' with a French accent. Then I'd be the 'Pink Flamingo in Australia.' "

Once he was in a position to be able to write his own ticket, he lost no time in moving. He bought *The End*, a black-humor script that had been written for Woody Allen, about a man who finds out he has a terminal illness. It was a part Burt would never have been cast in if it had been left to the studio heads, and it enabled him to take his first serious plunge into the field of directing.

"This will be a big departure for me," he said of his new venture with pride. "I won't drive over thirty-five miles an hour and I won't take off my shirt. It's very easy for me to make little-boy films where I chase the sheriffs and cops and run them off Alabama roads. I do that as well as anyone else around, but I would like to grow as an actor. I haven't taken a chance in a long time, partly because the scripts that land on my desk are not exactly Al Pacino scripts."

What made the step that much more enticing to Reynolds, who says he only enjoys skating if the ice is thin, is that the movie revolved around the forbidden subject of death. "It's the one thing nobody wants to talk about and what we are all going to do. If Onassis and Hughes couldn't buy their way out, nobody can," he said. "How marvelous it is to say it out loud and laugh about it. When you're twenty-five and thirty, you're immortal. But when you get to be forty, it does cross your mind. I read the obituaries now."

Part of the attraction the script held for Reynolds was its depiction of frightening experiences that were similar to his own. After working himself into a state of exhaustion by doing twenty-four films nearly back to back in a twelve-year period, his health collapsed, causing him to be rushed to the hospital numerous times for everything from false heart attacks to bleeding ulcers. He fainted on sets, was propped up between takes, and, desperate to find out what was wrong with him, explored everything from hypnosis to TM. He says he got so weak he forgot his mantra, and when he called the meditation center to ask for it, they couldn't give it to him on the phone. All they could do was tell him it was something about an automobile and cheerfulness, so he staggered around muttering "Happy Fender" under his breath.

He was finally diagnosed as having three different conditions—hyperventilation, a little-known condition called "Tietze's Syndrome," and a very bad case of hypoglycemia, which is treatable by diet. Before this, one of his trips to the hospital was right out of *The End*.

"I was tired, depressive, hyperventilating, fainting all the time. During that year some hysterical things happened. One night my heart started pounding so hard I thought my chest was caving in. So I called an ambulance. Now I'm on so many movie-star maps that everybody in Hollywood knows where my house is. Every tourist from Kokomo can find it, but this ambulance couldn't find it. They passed three times, so I dragged myself out on the lawn and waved at them and they went by again. So I lay down in the street until they stopped.

"We got to the hospital and they pumped something into my veins and shoved me into a room with three old Jewish guys playing cards. I was almost unconscious at this point when suddenly I felt a hand tapping against the intravenous bottle. I looked up and this old guy said, 'You play gin rummy?' I said, 'I'm dying.' To which he replied, 'We're all dying.' So we all ended up in wheelchairs playing cards while the nurse asked me for an autograph. Looking back, I realize that's as funny as a Mel Brooks movie, but I was terrified and very sick at the time. There can be humor in death, and dignity, too."

The End was a project that meant a lot to Burt, and he strived to be the best director he could, just as he had applied himself to everything else he had ever done. His efforts were handsomely rewarded, as everyone in the cast—Joanne Woodward, Myrna Loy, Sally Field, Pat O'Brien, and Dom DeLuise—can attest. All had praise that resounded with superlatives. Myrna Loy stated he was the most impressive director she had worked with in fifteen years. Sally Field said he drew her out as an actress as no other director ever had.

Dom DeLuise enthused, "He's marvelous. He's spontaneous. Everyone thinks of him as a sex symbol, a star, a stud—but he is a gentle, understanding, extremely tal-

ented director. One day he wanted me to go straight through a fifteen-page scene. Fifteen pages in one take! That frightened me. But he said, 'Listen, we can take three days. You have three days on it, so relax.' I believed him and my anxiety started to slip away—and, as it turned out, we got through it in one day."

Reynolds may have learned some of his directing skills by taking the opposite tack from many of the directors he worked with. "I may not be an expert on good words but I am on bad directors, and I've had my share of directors who should be directing traffic—maybe."

On *The End*, he said, the director had his share of problems, and forgot to take some of his close-ups, but other than that, he was good. "I trusted that director on *The End* more than any director I've ever worked with."

Most of Burt's movies, like *W.W. and the Dixie Dancekings,* show him as a "good ol' boy" from the South.

The rumor is that Sally and Burt will come back from Europe, where they will film *Smokey II,* as husband and wife.

15/WHAT THE FUTURE HOLDS

After Burt and Dinah split up, Burt spent some time dating around, but he quickly came to realize that that wasn't what he wanted out of life. The friends whose lives he admired the most were the ones who had happy homes and marriages, and he became increasingly aware of the emptiness in that area of his life.

He surprised all those who considered him a Casanova by announcing, "I'm ready to get married. I know I have a playboy image but that's not the real me. I've always basically been a one-woman man. I've never enjoyed playing the field. I keep thinking that special lady I'm looking for is right around the corner. I have this feeling that something is about to happen, that I may look up and see That Girl running across the field," he said, no pun intended.

Not long after, he and Sally Field became constant companions on and off screen. She has been his leading lady in his last three pictures, *Smokey and the Bandit*, *The End*, and *Hooper*.

Although Burt has maintained his tradition of not talking about the woman in his life beyond the broadest generalities, their relationship seems to speak for itself. Many in Hollywood call them the new Gable and Lombard, partly because Reynolds has a lot in common with Gable, and partly because their romance has been going on intensely for two years, without a marriage license. Most of all, though, the way they are with each other—relaxed, affectionate, full of fun—reminds many people of how Gable and Lombard were with each other before her untimely death.

The bond that exists between Sally and Burt is intimated in *Hooper*. The characters they portrayed in that movie reflect their own relationship, its warmth and commitment and deep understanding.

In a rare statement to the press, Reynolds said, "She's the only girl I've ever known who loves me—and lets me feel free at the same time." He explains that some of the other things that draw him to her are her terrific sense of humor and childlike quality. She rejoins by saying

The Silver Screen Archives

Burt and Sally at *Side by Side by Sondheim* in New York.

that they have a lot in common, being old-fashioned, shy, and having worked through bad self-images. One of the fibers that has given strength to their relationship has been the support they have been able to give each other in the new directions they are taking in their careers.

After making the first important break with a career that, like Burt's, had been stifled by typecasting, Sally Field is on her way to becoming one of the most important actresses in this country. It took a lot of hard work and courage to break loose from the stereotype of *Gidget* and *The Flying Nun*, but her stunning Emmy-winning performance in *Sybil* established her in one stroke as a tremendously accomplished actress. With the recently re-

leased *Norma Rae*, also starring Ron Leibman and Beau Bridges, and directed by Martin Ritt, her place as a serious actress of great importance is assured.

This fall, Burt and Sally will go to Europe to make *Smokey and the Bandit II* and many say they will come back man and wife. Although he has remained afraid to marry again because of his failure with Judy, Burt has also said, "I must admit I feel the nesting urge coming on very strong. I'm ready to get married again. I know I have a playboy image, but that's not the real me. I have the feeling that something is about to happen . . . and I suppose that something could be marriage."

One reason Reynolds wants to marry is

so that he can settle down and have a family, and that this is a good reason to override his fear.

"I'm petrified of failure," he explained. "I'm no good at failure. I'm good at success. I'm a terrific front-runner, but you let me lose and I'm not good at that.

"I gave it everything I had when I was married before and it didn't work. So I'm very afraid of marriage, but I'd still like to have a family and all those things," he explained.

"I think I would be a very good father," he added. "I'm crazy about kids and I like to have a lot of them around me, sharing things.

"Every week at the ranch I have a hundred kids there. They come from all over the neighborhood—but they're not mine."

Burt has a ready-made family in Sally's

The National Association of Theater Owners honored Burt for being the number-one box-office draw in the country.

Burt hasn't had to use that "panic button" but it's always nice to have it close at hand.

two boys, Peter, 8, and Eli, 6.

There are many reasons why the $25,000 diamond brooch he gave her to mark the beginning of their third film together may have secretly pledged a lot more.

One thing is certain. Their relationship is a tremendously meaningful one to both of them. If they decide to make their commitment a legal one, it will come as no surprise to anyone.

Life is very good these days for Burt. At this point in his career and personal life, he has just about everything he had ever hoped to have.

"I'll be a wonderful old man. I've had a very full life," he says with great satisfaction. I've never bad-mouthed being a movie star—I've enjoyed every minute of it. You get away with even more when you're older. The stories you have to tell sound even better. And I'll have some stories to tell."

While Burt is happy with the way things

have turned out for him, he hasn't lost any of his zest and spirit of adventure. He always wants to know what's around the next corner. He wants to write, learn to play the piano, take flying lessons, and learn other languages.

In his career, he wants to take more and more risks, broaden himself as an actor, then home in on directing—which is what he would like to do fulltime eventually. "I'd like to lead a quiet life and just direct two pictures a year. After all, you can hold your stomach in for just so long," he says.

Reynolds puts his money where his mouth is. He sank $1 million of his own money into *The End*. He gets twice that just to star in a picture, but the risk was worth it to break out of the mold he was trapped in.

With *Starting Over*, also starring Jill Clayburgh and Candice Bergen, Burt is moving toward the kinds of movies he does want to make now, which will be

Burt hopes to be in a movie with Jane Fonda someday, but his commitments go well into 1982. Warren Beatty rounds out this threesome.

Burt and Sally have been together over two years now. They have a lot in common; both have had to surmount tremendous difficulties in getting their careers off the ground.

more like "Cary Grant movies" than "Burt Reynolds movies." "I want to make romantic movies about neat people," he says ingenuously.

In the past, Reynolds felt he had to adjust himself somewhat to the demands of a burgeoning career. Now that he is on top, he doesn't have to do that anymore.

"I'm no longer prepared to do things to preserve my so-called image. The hell with that. If I want to eat spaghetti in public and get it all over me, I'll do it.

There was a time when I wouldn't have. I'd have been worried in case someone came over to the table and said, 'Listen, I'm really disappointed to see you eating spaghetti so sloppily. From now on I won't see any more of your pictures.'"

Laughing softly, he added, "If that happened today, you know who'd wind up with the spaghetti."

He who laughs last, laughs loudest, and Reynolds has a lot to laugh about these days.

The relationship between the characters Burt and Sally play in *Hooper* was based on their own real feelings for each other.